BE ART. BE TRUE. BE YOU.

Copyright © 2024 Laura Henkel

All rights reserved. No part of this book may be reproduced, stored in a retrieval system, or transmitted in any form or by any means, electronic, mechanical, photocopying, recording, or otherwise, without the prior written permission of the author.

Consistency and authenticity are your secret weapons. Show up, stand out, and let your passion shine!

Table of Contents

01	The Author
02	Introduction
03	Discovering Your Voice
04	Building Your Portfolio
05	Networking and Building Relationships
06	Showcasing Your Art
07	Marketing and Selling Your Art
08	Maximizing Social Media for Art Marketing
09	Managing Finances on a Budget
10	Staying Motivated and Inspired
11	Conclusion

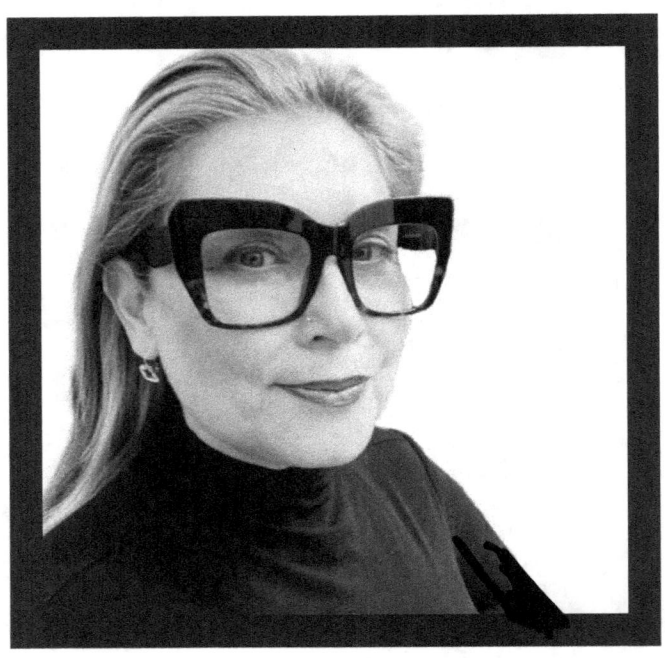

ARTCULTUREPR.COM

N.1 The Author

Dr. Laura Henkel is a renowned expert with over two decades of experience seamlessly integrating arts and commerce to significantly boost stakeholder engagement. As the Founder and Managing Director of ArtCulture PR, she boasts a proven track record in managing operations while navigating diverse cultural landscapes. She excels in crafting bespoke business strategies to achieve sustainable growth and remarkable success for complex, multidisciplinary projects. Her marketing prowess is a cornerstone of her expertise, enabling her to elevate the profiles of creatives and arts and cultural organizations. Beyond her consulting achievements, Dr. Laura has directed museums, owned a gallery, and established an internationally recognized art festival, as well as curated global exhibitions and public art installations on behalf of her clients. Her initiatives have launched the careers of numerous artists and organizations. Dr. Laura continues to champion the arts both locally and globally. She also writes for prominent arts and culture publications, sharing her insights and expertise with a wider audience. Her leadership and vision have consistently driven creative enterprises toward unparalleled success, solidifying her reputation as a leading authority in her field.

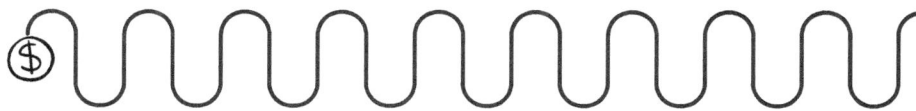

N.2 Introduction

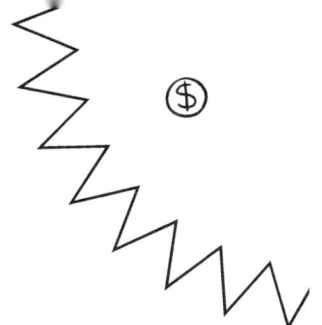

Welcome to *"Breaking into the Art World on a Budget: A Practical Guide for Emerging Artists"*! This DIY guide will help you build your art business by creating a strong foundation and mechanisms to care for your interests for years to come.

I'm Dr. Laura Henkel, and I'm thrilled to share this journey with you. My career has been dedicated to elevating the profiles of creatives and arts organizations through strategic marketing, directing museums, owning Sin City Gallery, and establishing the internationally recognized art festival, 12 Inches of Sin. As the Founder and Managing Director of ArtCulture PR, I've launched the careers of artists and art organizations, curating global exhibitions and public art installations. I've also been retained to restructure art organizations, transforming them into thriving entities based on these strategies. I've been there, done that, and worn many hats. That's why I have written this guide.

This guide is my desire to share my knowledge and expertise with emerging artists, helping you make your mark in the art world and enjoy your careers in the process by providing a business blueprint for success. For established artists and art organizations, this guide also serves as a wonderful refresher. It is easy to be distracted or seek instant gratification, but slow and steady wins the race. Once you have created a blueprint for your own business endeavors, stay the course. By doing so, you will notice it provides you more time to create and less time dedicated to business because you have created a system that supports you, not the other way around.

The information found in this guide is designed to help emerging artists like you navigate the complexities of the art world, showcase your talent, and build a successful career without breaking the bank. By following the strategies outlined in this resource, you can achieve your artistic goals, stay true to your vision, and create a sustainable and fulfilling career in the arts. Let's embark on this exciting journey together, and I look forward to seeing the amazing work you'll accomplish!

N.3 Discovering Your Voice

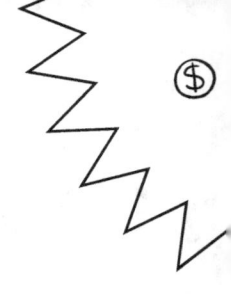

3.1 Embrace Your Individuality
Identify what makes your art unique by reflecting on your personal experiences, cultural background, and the themes that resonate with you. Consider the artists, movements, or life events that have shaped your work. This reflection can help you understand your artistic lineage and develop a distinct voice.

3.2 Develop a Consistent Style
Experiment with different mediums and techniques to find what feels most natural and expressive for you. Once you identify your preferred style, focus on creating a series of pieces that reflect this style. Consistency will help you build a recognizable brand.

3.3 Set Clear Goals
Define what success looks like for you, whether it's recognition, sales, or personal fulfillment. Set short-term and long-term goals for your artistic career, such as finishing a new series of artworks or having a solo exhibition.

N.4 Building Your Portflio

4.1 Curate Your Best Work
Select pieces that best represent your abilities and artistic voice, focusing on quality over quantity. Ensure your portfolio is diverse yet cohesive, showcasing a unified vision.

4.2 Create a Digital Portfolio
Use affordable platforms like Artfinder, Artsy, Etsy, Saatchi, and Singular to showcase your artwork. Additionally, create your own website via Squarespace, Wix, or WordPress to develop a user-friendly digital portfolio. Include high-quality images, an artist statement, and contact information. Ensure your portfolio is optimized for both desktop and mobile viewing.

4.3 Print Portfolio
Invest in high-quality prints of your work and create a professional and portable physical portfolio. Use a sleek, durable portfolio case and include business cards and a résumé for in-person opportunities.

N.5 Networking and Building Relationships

5.1 Attend Art Events
Participate in local art shows, exhibitions, and festivals to meet fellow artists, collectors, and gallery owners. Volunteering at art organizations can open doors to new connections.

5.2 Join Online Art Communities
Engage on social media platforms like Instagram, Twitter, and Facebook groups to network and share your work. Contribute to online forums and art critique groups like Reddit's art subreddits or DeviantArt for feedback and discussions.

N.6 Showcasing Your Art

5.3 Collaborate with Other Artists
Work on joint projects or group exhibitions to introduce your work to new audiences and provide mutual support. Share resources and promote each other's work to expand your reach and build a stronger community.

6.1 Find Affordable Venues
Exhibit your work in local cafes, libraries, and community centers. Participate in open studio events and art fairs to showcase your work in person.

- **Art Collectives and Co-Working Spaces**: Join local collectives for gallery space and networking.

- **Art Fairs and Festivals**: Participate in local events for high visibility at low cost.

- **Art Walks and Open Studios**: Open your studio to the public during local events.

- **Colleges and Universities**: Reach out to faculty members or gallery coordinators.

- **Corporate Offices and Businesses**: Contact companies or work with art consultants.

- **Galleries**: Research galleries that align with your art. Attend their exhibitions to understand their curatorial approach and get to know the gallery curators. Building a relationship with curators is essential; approach them at appropriate times, avoiding opening or closing receptions, to discuss your work. Cultivate relationships organically, allowing opportunities to present your work to arise naturally through mutual interest and understanding.

- **Libraries and Community Centers**: Inquire about exhibition schedules and submission guidelines.

- **Local Cafes and Restaurants**: Approach owners with a professional portfolio to display your work for free.

- **Partner with Non-Profit Organizations**: Host exhibitions that align with their missions.

- **Pop-Up Galleries and Shops**: Look for vacant retail spaces or collaborate with other artists.

- **Public Spaces and Outdoor Exhibitions**: Collaborate with local governments for permits.

To support you on your journey, you may find additional opportunities to expand your reach, gain recognition, and secure new projects. Here is a listing of several organizations that provide up-to-date listings of art contests, exhibitions, residencies, and grants worldwide:

- **ArtCall.org**: Known for its call for entry management system, it also provides extensive listings of art contests and events with filters for easier browsing.

- **ArtDeadline.com**: Pioneer online resource featuring thousands of listings for art opportunities, many of which are free to view. Paid subscriptions offer exclusive access to additional listings.

- **Artjobs.com**: Features a comprehensive open calls section for the arts and creative fields, with free and paid registration options.

- **Artshow**: Features information on online art contests, residencies, exhibitions, and festivals. Tutorials and workshops are available for artists of all skill levels.

- **Burnaway**: Digital magazine focused on art and literature from the American South. Provides monthly updated calls for artists, along with reviews and interviews.

- **C4E (Call for Entries)**: Offers searchable directories, updated weekly with information on art calls and photography calls globally. Free registration provides access to newsletters and exclusive listings.

- **callforentry.org (CaFÉ)**: Created by WESTAF, it offers sorted call listings for easy browsing and a streamlined application process.

- **Contest Watchers**: Extensive database of international competitions in various artistic disciplines, updated daily. Listings are grouped by category for easy navigation.

- **CuratorSpace**: Project management service for curators and artists offering multiple pages of listings for various artistic opportunities.

- **Dark Yellow Dot**: Based in London, it offers opportunities for new and seasoned artists to participate in art contests, exhibitions, and fellowships.

- **EntryThingy**: Regularly updated listings of art competitions throughout the United States. Offers an Artwork Management account for easier application processes.

- **International Competitions**: Lists global art contests with comprehensive details on eligibility, entry fees, and prizes. Also includes contests in writing, film, and photography.

- **Side Arts**: Global community for visual artists to promote their work and find verified calls for artists. Offers free and paid membership options.

- **TheArtGuide.com**: Comprehensive resource for calls for entry, art contests, festivals, and exhibits. Offers free and premium memberships.

- **TheArtList.com**: Provides listings of online art contests, residencies, exhibitions, and festivals with tutorials on various art forms.

- **ZAPP**: Facilitates applications to American art fairs, shows, and festivals. Free registration provides access to a comprehensive online application process.

6.2 Virtual Exhibitions

Host virtual exhibitions and live-stream your art process using tools like Zoom or Instagram Live. Virtual exhibitions can significantly enhance your reach and engagement. Here is a listing of virtual exhibition platforms to also consider:

- **Accelevents**: Includes customizable exhibit halls, a booth exhibitor dashboard, and advanced sponsorship options.

- **Dreamcast**: Features a DIY booth builder and strong communication integrations.

- **EventX**: Provides a reliable hosting platform with virtual booths, live streaming, and lead capture features.

- **Hexafair**: Known for its immersive 3D experiences, ticketing, and robust event branding options.

- **Pheedloop**: Known for customizable exhibit booths, interactive floor plans, and extensive sponsorship options.

- **Remo**: Delivers virtual environments that mimic real-world interactions with customizable booths and effective networking tools.

- **RingCentral (formerly Hopin)**: Features customizable exhibit booths, sponsorship visibility, and event analytics.

- **Swapcard**: Provides virtual booths, interactive webinars, event statistics, and lead capture.

- **vFairs**: Offers comprehensive event management features, customizable virtual environments, advanced networking capabilities, interactive exhibit halls, and document hosting.

- **Whova**: Offers interactive exhibit booths, networking, gamification tools, and lead capture capabilities.

6.2 Leverage Online Platforms
Use Instagram, Etsy, and other online marketplaces to reach a wider audience. Host virtual exhibitions and live-stream your art process using tools like Zoom or Instagram Live.

6.4 Showcase Your Artwork on Online Marketplaces
Use platforms like Artfinder, Artsy, Etsy, Saatchi, and Singular.

6.5 Create Your Own Website
In addition to using online marketplaces, create your own website to develop a user-friendly digital portfolio. Include high-quality images, an artist statement, and contact information. Ensure your portfolio is optimized for both desktop and mobile viewing.

If you think that using a website is outdated, think again! Having a dedicated website for your art practice offers numerous advantages compared to or in addition to using online marketplaces.

Here are the benefits:

- **Full Ownership**: Complete control over content, design, and functionality.

- **Customization**: Unique brand identity with custom designs, layouts, and features.

- **No Restrictions**: No content limitations, allowing full artistic expression.

- **Direct Traffic**: Drive traffic through SEO, social media, email marketing, and other strategies.

- **Analytics**: Use tools like Google Analytics to understand visitor behavior and refine marketing strategies.

- **Email List**: Build and maintain an email list for direct communication and promotions.
- **E-commerce Integration**: Sell artwork directly from your site, managing sales, inventory, and customer relationships.
- **Lower Fees**: Potentially lower transaction fees compared to third-party platform commissions.
- **Building a Community**: Create a blog, forum, or membership section for personal engagement and community building.
- **Collaboration Opportunities**: Use your site as a hub for collaborations with other artists, galleries, or institutions.
- **Professional Image**: Enhance your professional image with a well-designed website showcasing your portfolio, biography, and press coverage.
- **Comprehensive Showcase**: Provide a detailed view of your work, including high-resolution images, videos, and descriptions.

Combining both online marketplaces and a website can maximize your reach and effectiveness, leveraging the strengths of each to support your goals. Be sure to weigh the pros and cons of using both resources for your needs. Start with one. You can always add the one-two punch later.

6.6 Social Media Integration

Integrate your online presence with social media platforms. Share updates, behind-the-scenes content, and engage with your audience on Instagram, Facebook, Pinterest, Twitter, and TikTok. Planoly can help you manage and disseminate content across these channels while also offering e-commerce capabilities.

N.7 Marketing and Selling Your Art

7.1 Pricing Your Artwork
Research market rates for similar art and consider your time, materials, and overhead costs. Ensure your pricing covers all expenses and provides a fair profit margin.

7.2 Create a Marketing Plan
Use social media to promote your art by regularly posting images of your work, studio shots, and process videos. Build an email list to keep your audience updated on new work and upcoming events.

7.3 Sales Channels
Sell directly through your website or online marketplaces like Big Cartel, Etsy, Planoly, or Shopify. Approach galleries and local shops about consignment or representation to increase your exposure.

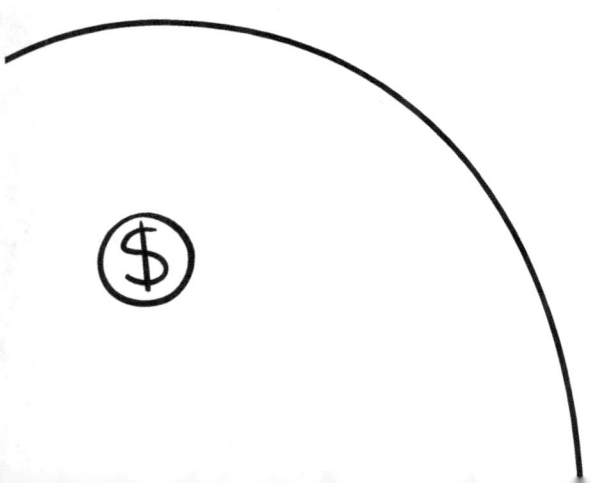

N.8 Maximizing Social Media for Art Marketing

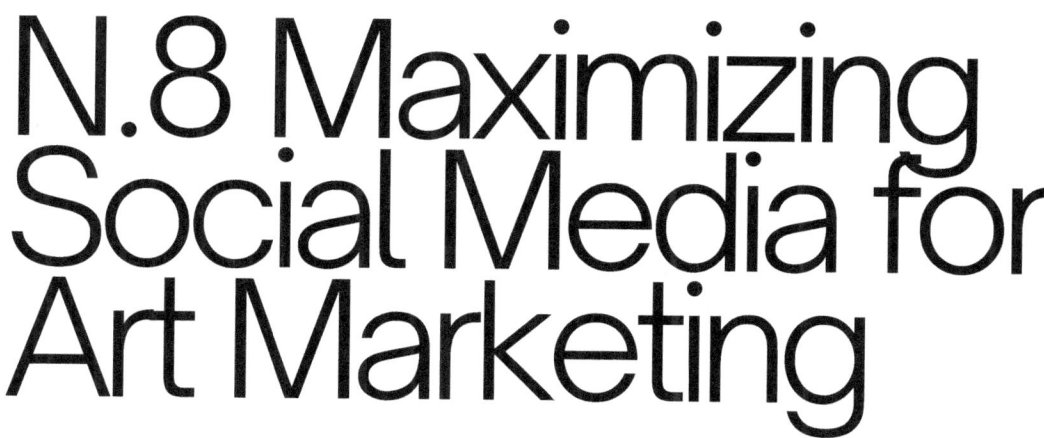

8.1 Choosing the Right Platforms
Select platforms that best suit your art and audience. Instagram is ideal for visual artists, while Facebook is great for creating a business page and promoting events. Pinterest can drive traffic to your website, Twitter is perfect for networking, and TikTok is excellent for short-form videos showcasing your process. Planoly is an excellent tool not only for disseminating content across your various social media channels but also for selling directly on the platform.

8.1 Choosing the Right Platforms
Select platforms that best suit your art and audience. Instagram is ideal for visual artists, while Facebook is great for creating events or promoting a business page. Pinterest can drive traffic to your website, Twitter is perfect for networking, and TikTok is excellent for short-form videos showcasing your process. Planoly is an excellent tool not only for disseminating content across your various social media channels but also for selling directly on the platform.

8.2 Creating Engaging Content
Invest time in photographing your artwork in good lighting and use editing tools to enhance the quality. Share behind-the-scenes content, artist stories, and interactive content like polls, Q&A sessions, and live streams to engage your audience.

8.3 Building a Consistent Brand
Maintain a consistent style in your posts, develop a regular posting schedule, and create a unique and authentic voice for your captions and interactions.

8.4 Utilizing Social Media Tools
Use built-in analytics to track engagement and audience demographics. Schedule posts in advance with tools like Planoly, Buffer, or Later. Research and use relevant hashtags to increase visibility.

8.5 Engaging with Your Audience
Respond to comments and messages to build a loyal community. Partner with influencers or other artists for cross-promotion and host giveaways and contests to increase engagement.

8.6 Promoting Sales and Events
Promote your online store for upcoming exhibitions, and workshops. Create urgency with limited-time offers and exclusive deals for your followers.

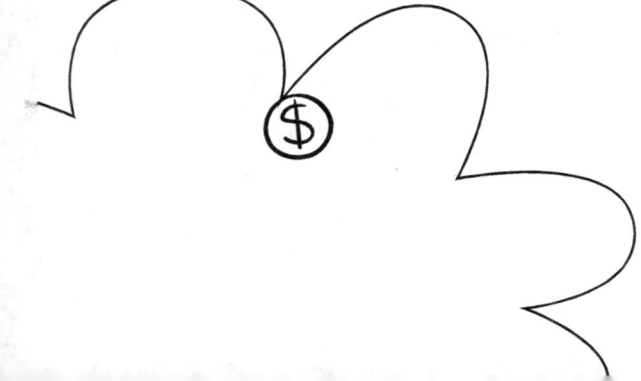

N.9 Managing Finances on a Budget

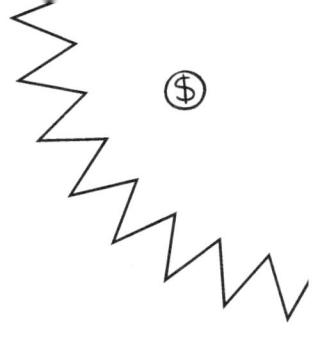

9.1 Budgeting for Artists
Track your income and expenses using budgeting apps or spreadsheets. Plan for irregular income and set aside funds for taxes.

9.2 DIY Marketing Materials
Create your own business cards, flyers, and promotional materials using tools like Canva. Utilize free online resources for design templates to save on costs.

9.3 Continuing Education
Take advantage of free or low-cost online courses on platforms like Coursera, Udemy, and Skillshare. Attend local community college classes or art workshops to enhance your skills and knowledge.

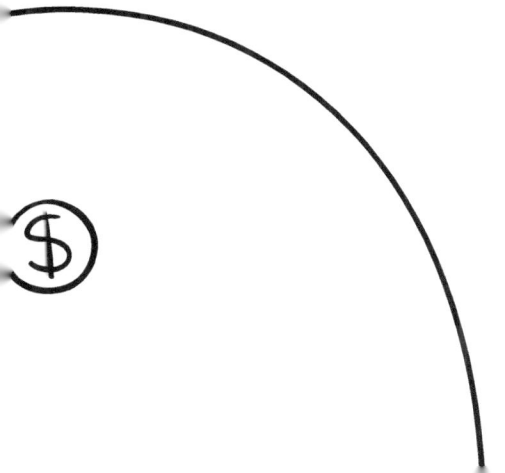

N.10 Staying Motivated and Inspired

10.1 Setting Up Your Creative Space
Create a dedicated workspace that inspires you, whether it's a corner of a room or a full studio. Organize your materials and tools for efficiency to foster creativity.

10.2 Overcoming Creative Blocks
Practice daily sketching or journaling to spark new ideas. Take breaks and seek inspiration from nature, music, or other art forms to rejuvenate your creativity.

10.3 Building a Support System
Surround yourself with supportive friends and fellow artists. Seek feedback and encouragement from your art community to help you grow as an artist.

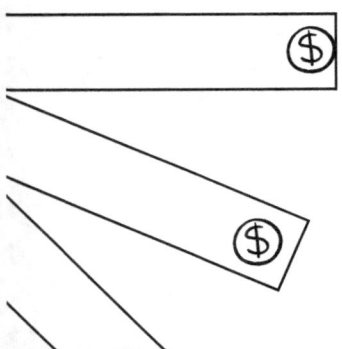

N.10 Staying Motivated and Inspired

10.1 Setting Up Your Creative Space
Create a dedicated workspace that inspires you, whether it's a corner of a room or a full studio. Organize your materials and tools for efficiency to foster creativity.

10.2 Overcoming Creative Blocks
Practice daily sketching or journaling to spark new ideas. Take breaks and seek inspiration from nature, music, or other art forms to rejuvenate your creativity.

10.3 Building a Support System
Surround yourself with supportive friends and fellow artists. Seek feedback and encouragement from your art community to help you grow as an artist.

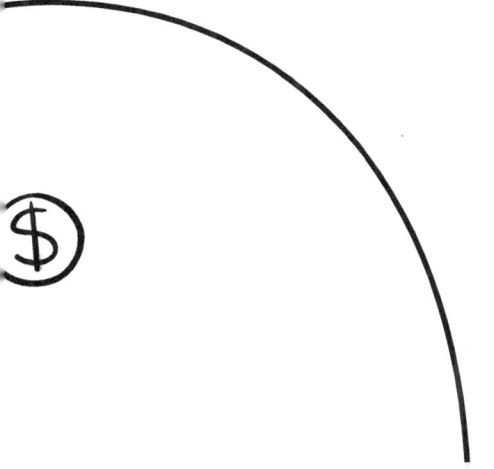

N.11 Conclusion

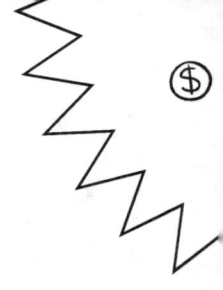

As we conclude this guide, I hope you feel inspired, empowered, and ready to embark on your artistic journey. The strategies and resources shared here are designed to help you build a strong foundation for your art business, as well as to explore and grow.

Your creativity is your greatest asset, and with the right tools and strategies, you can achieve remarkable success. Embrace the journey, stay true to your art, and let your passion shine. I look forward to seeing the incredible work you'll create and the impact you'll make in the art world.

Remember, your unique experiences, perspectives, and desires are vital to your creative process and success. They shape your art and distinguish your work in the crowded landscape of the art world.

This guide provides actionable advice and practical steps to help you embrace your creativity, stay true to your vision, and achieve lasting success. Your journey to a rewarding and impactful art career starts here.

You Got This!

Dr. Laura

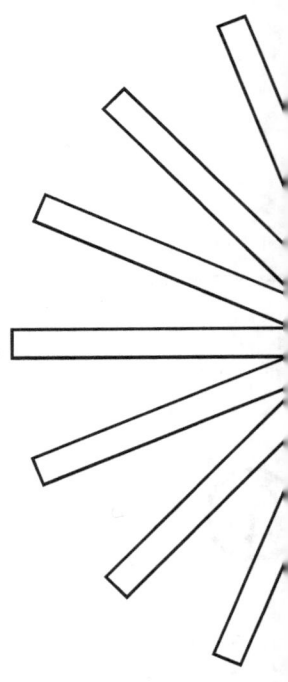

www.ingramcontent.com/pod-product-compliance
Lightning Source LLC
Chambersburg PA
CBHW062210220526
45470CB00009B/2992